ENID BLYTON

at Old Thatch

Tess Livingstone
(Pictures: Matthew Rose)

© Copyright, Tess Livingstone, 2008, 2012

All Rights Reserved

Published by
Connor Court Publishing, 2008.
PO BOX 1
BALLAN VIC 3342
www.connorcourt.com
Phone (03) 5368 2570
Fax (03) 5303 0960

ISBN: 978-1-921421-03-7

Quotes reproduced by kind permission of Chorion Rights Limited. All rights reserved.

ENID BLYTON ® is a registered trade mark of Chorion Rights Limited. All rights reserved.

Photographs in this book by Matthew Rose, except where indicated. All rights reserved.

Front cover photo of Old Thatch in Autumn by Matthew Rose

Back cover photo of Old Thatch in Winter by Jacky and David Hawthorne

Cover design by Brigid Cappello

*This book is dedicated to Gail and Elley
with love and a "big thank you" for so many happy times*

Also in memory of Gillian Baverstock

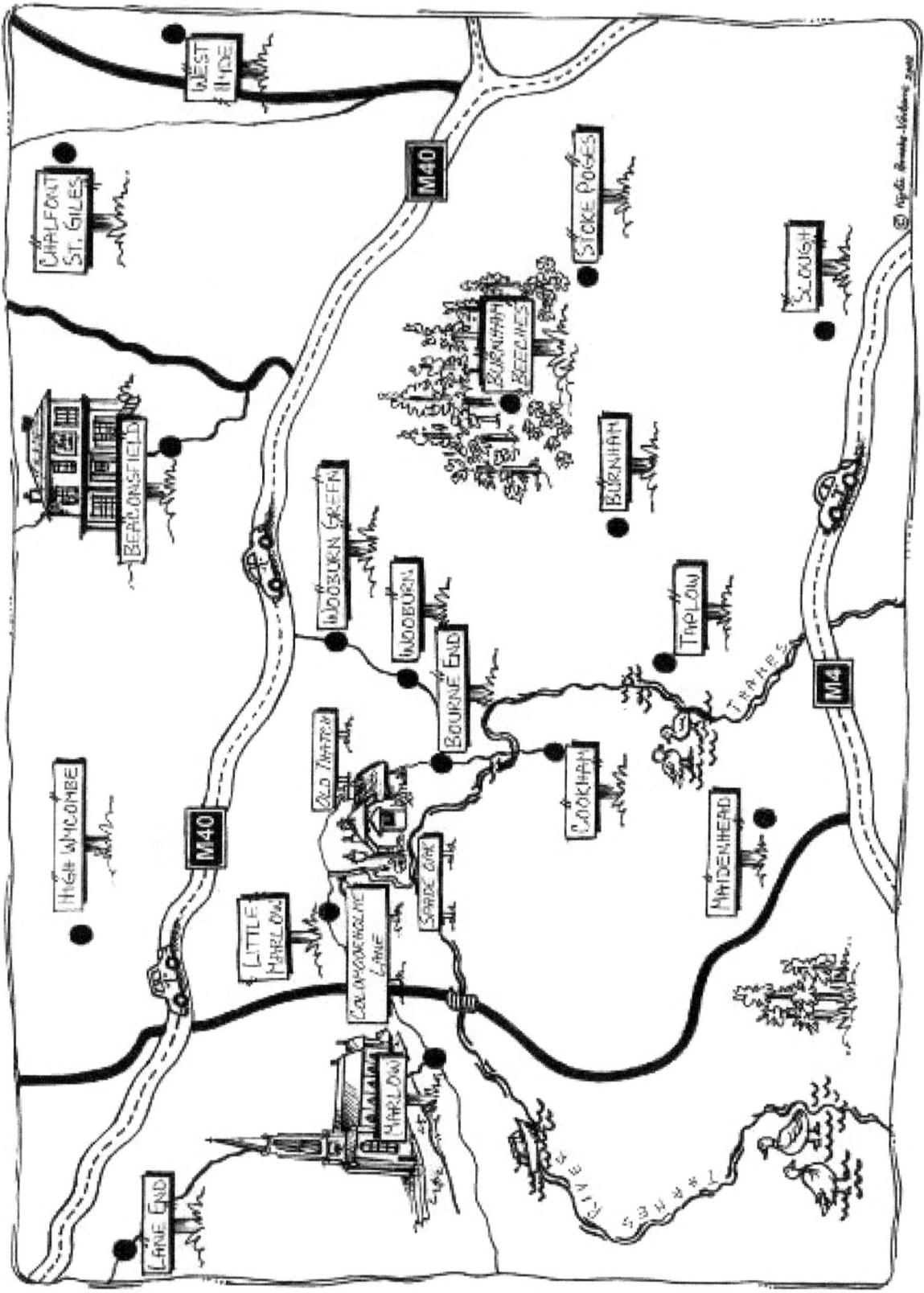

Table of Contents

Chapter One:
Starting at Old Thatch   1

Chapter Two:
Stepping through the open door to Peterswood   10

Chapter Three:
Places real .... and almost real   25

Chapter Four:
Down a storybook lane   37

Chapter Five:
Back in the real world   41

Chapter Six
Hidden Treasure   56

Acknowledgements   62

How it all Began   63

Footnotes   66

Chapter One
Starting at *Old Thatch*

It looks like a fairy tale house, but it is real and special. *Old Thatch* is a 17th century thatched home - too impressive to be called a "cottage" - on the banks of the Thames, about 40 kms west of London in Coldmoorholme Lane, Bourne End, Buckinghamshire. It is a perfect setting to inspire a writer with a vivid imagination, which is one reason children's author Enid Blyton penned many of her most memorable stories here. *Old Thatch* was Enid Blyton's home from 1929 to 1938, and where her two daughters, Gillian and Imogen, were born.

As Blyton related in *"The Story of My Life"*, *Old Thatch* appealed to her because it was "exactly like a house in a fairy-tale of long ago." It appeared in many of her books when the story called for a cottage or an inn. She had a strong sense that her time in the home was just a snippet of its long, fascinating history.

"It had once been a cosy little inn called the Rose and Crown, and many people had been happy there," Blyton wrote. "For that reason I used to think the house had a lovely feel to it – friendly, happy, welcoming. It had an old well with a bucket to wind up and down, it had hidden treasure that nobody could ever find, and it even had a 'ghost'."

"There was a beautiful lych gate, with a thatched roof of its own, for a front entrance to the garden. There were thousands of crocuses in the springtime. There was a pond where the water-hens nested every year, bringing up families of busy little chicks, bobbing merrily up and down on the water." [1]

The garden also had "several fine old yew trees and an orchard with apples and pears in abundance," Blyton wrote in her magazine, *Letter to Children*. She described "a large, somewhat overgrown lily pond, a rosewalk, a kitchen garden 'with everything growing there that you could possibly want', a small wood and a brook 'with a little bridge of its own'." [2]

Old Thatch and its surrounds experience the best of the four seasons – riverside fun in summer, leafy autumns, cosy firesides on wintry days and spring blossoms. A keen gardener who wrote numerous gardening and nature books for children, including *Hedgerow Tales* and *Let's Garden*, Blyton would delight in the beauty of the *Old Thatch* gardens today. This important piece of heritage is being well cared for and enhanced by current owners, Jacky and David Hawthorne, who have lavished care and attention on the house since they bought it in 1994. It has never looked better and has recently been re-thatched with reed, designed to last a century.

Old Thatch is worth a visit on weekend and Bank Holiday afternoons in late spring and summer, when the Hawthornes open it up for those who enjoy a good ramble around an exquisite English country garden followed by "tea and scrummy cake". A garden designer by profession, Jacky Hawthorne has weaved her creative magic across the two acres, resulting in *Old Thatch* being awarded one-star status in the Telegraph Good Gardens Guide from 2008. To put that honour in context, two stars is the only other accolade awarded under the scheme, and that goes to gardens of stately homes covering hundreds of acres.

The highly coveted star puts *Old Thatch* in the top seven percent of gardens open to the public in the British Isles and Ireland, another good reason for visiting it aside from the Blyton connection. Given the imagination and skill

Jacky Hawthorne has used in breathing new life into the garden, it is not surprising that her services are in strong demand from residents across Buckinghamshire, Berkshire, Oxfordshire and west London. See **www.jackyhawthorne.co.uk.**

Another "must see" for Blyton fans is the Enid Blyton room at the Red Lion pub, Knotty Green, Beaconsfield, four miles away. Initiated by Bob and Tina Massie (yes, Aussie cricket fans will smile), the room's books and prints were donated by members of the Enid Blyton society - which can be found at: **www.enidblytonsociety.co.uk.**
The room is listed in the Buckinghamshire Tourism Guide: **www.visitbuckinghamshire.org/site/literary-connections.** Enid Blyton and her family moved to "Green Hedges" in Beaconsfield after leaving *Old Thatch*.

Even many Bourne End residents who number themselves as Blyton fans do not realise that the author set one of her most popular, and many would argue her best, series of children's novels in their village and surrounds. More than 60 years after it first appeared, the "Mystery" series, published from 1943 to 1961, still sells around 800,000 copies a year around the world in dozens of languages.

The 180-page books first appeared in different-coloured hardcovers, with a magnifying glass and fingerprint in the corners. Wrapped around each book was a well-illustrated dust jacket. Intact first and early editions are eagerly sought after, with prices soaring.

To a certain extent, the Mystery series was overshadowed by the phenomenal popularity of the Famous Five books about a different group of children (Julian, Dick, Anne, George and Timmy the dog) which owed many of their settings to another part of England – Dorset, where Enid Blyton and her family often holidayed.
For those keen to follow that trail, author Vivienne Endecott sets it out well in *The Dorset Days of Enid Blyton* (**www.gingerpop.co.uk**). Blyton devotees would also enjoy The Ginger Pop Shop in the Square in Corfe, Dorset, where Vivienne sells all manner of Blyton books and memorabilia, and in true Blyton style, "lashings" of ginger pop.

An intriguing ceiling... inside Old Thatch (Picture: Jacky and David Hawthorne)

Popular as the *Famous Five* were, however, many regard the Mystery books as the cleverest, funniest and best plotted books Enid Blyton produced out of her 700 published works. The 15 children's novels featured a group of amateur child detectives who called themselves the "Five Find-Outers and Dog". They included Fatty, the genius head of the group whose wit, tricks and disguises enlivened the action, Larry the eldest, Daisy his sister, Pip and his younger sister Bets, along with Buster, Fatty's black Scottie. At the time the series starts, Larry was 13, Fatty, Pip and Daisy were 12 and Bets was 8. And unlike other Blyton series, the children grew older as the stories unfolded.

From *The Mystery of the Burnt Cottage*, the first in the series, through many more school holidays, the Find-Outers solved a raft of peculiar crime mysteries, outwitting the hapless local bobby, PC Goon, and raising plenty of laughs.

Peterswood, the fictitious village where the children lived, was based on Blyton's Bourne End. A settlement there was first mapped as "Burnend" in 1236, meaning "end of the stream", where the Bourne joins the Thames.

The Red Lion Pub (Picture: Tina and Bob Massie)

In the Mystery books, the local stream is referred to in **The Mystery of the Hidden House**. A local wood, with a closed-up house full of secrets in the middle, is Bourne Wood.[3]

In the main street of Bourne End, the road signposts point to names familiar to Find-Outer fans. And even for those who have never heard of the series, the signposts point (in miles) to some of south-east England's most interesting places and glorious countryside: Burnham Beeches 5; Cliveden 2; Beaconsfield (where Enid Blyton lived at Green Hedges after leaving Bourne End) 4; Marlow 3; Maidenhead 4; Taplow 2. All are close to the Buckinghamshire/Berkshire border in the Thames Valley, between the M4 (exit at Junctions 7, 8 or 9) and M40 (exit at Junctions 2, 3 or 4) Motorways.

Regardless of whether readers first encountered some of these place names in a Mystery book on the beach in Australia over the long, hot Christmas holidays, in one of India's teeming cities, on crowded London trains or in a foreign language, the signposts are a clue (or "glue" as Bets, the youngest Find-Outer used to say early in the series). A clue to what? A clue to the real world of the Mystery books, as well as a gateway to some "must see" locations.

Marlow Bridge

Many of the Find-Outer settings were part of the early childhood landscape of Gillian, Enid Blyton's elder daughter, who was seven when the family left Bourne End. In 2002, at her home in Ilkley, Yorkshire, where she had her mother's writing desk from Bourne End and her garden statue of a small girl absorbed in a book, Mrs Gillian Baverstock, by then a grandmother herself, recalled life in Bourne End. She drew numerous parallels between the childhood she remembered and what the Find-Outers did in the books.

One of her strongest memories of that much safer time was riding her bicycle to Burnham Beeches for picnics in spring. "May was the time to go, when the ground was carpeted in bluebells," Gillian recalled. Much of the ground is still carpeted in bluebells in May in what is one of Britain's most ancient woodlands, a 220 hectare (540 acre) haven for plants and wildlife, owned by the City of London Corporation. It is dominated by the vast beeches, which attract 500,000 visitors a year. For instructions on finding it, see **www.cityoflondon.gov.uk/Corporation/living_environment/open_spaces/burnham.htm.**

In the Mystery books, Burnham Beeches was a favourite Find-Outers picnic spot:

> "Let's take our lunch with us and go to Burnham Beeches," said Larry in **The Mystery of the Spiteful Letters.** "We'll have grand fun there, you should just see some of the beeches, Bets – enormous old giants all gnarled and knotted, and some of them really seem to have faces in their knotted old trunks!"
> "Oooh – I'd like to go," said Bets. "I'm big enough to ride all the way with you this year. Mummy wouldn't let me last year" when she had to be content with a bunch of primroses brought back from the excursion by Fatty in **The Mystery of the Burnt Cottage.**[4]

Gillian also recalled the real-life police Inspector – Stephen Jenkins from the nearby Buckinghamshire town of Gerrard's Cross – on whom her mother modelled Inspector Jenks, who appeared in all the Mystery books. "They were friends, she admired him and he admired the books and was tickled pink to be included," Gillian said. As her mother wrote in **The Mystery of the Missing Necklace**:

> Inspector Jenks was their very good friend. He was what Bets called "a very high-up policeman," and he belonged to the next big town. In the four mysteries the children had solved before, Inspector Jenks had come in at the end, and been very pleased indeed at all the children had found out. Mr Goon, however, had

not been so pleased, because it was most annoying to him to have those "interfering children messing about with the Law" – especially when they had actually found out things he hadn't.[5]

In the main, the Mystery books were a series of "who dunits?" Who burnt the cottage? Stole the Siamese cat? Hid the precious necklace? Sent the Strange Messages? The children also set out to get to the bottom of puzzling questions such as: What secrets are hidden in one barred upstairs room of the deserted Milton House in Chestnut Lane? Why did a tiny red boat in a valuable sea picture at Banshee Towers apparently disappear overnight – is it art fraud? Can the thief who leaves large footprints and gloveprints really be invisible? What was in the Strange Bundle? Are fraudsters hiding in Tally-Ho House or cottage? Such questions kept them and millions of readers occupied in school holidays for years.

Entering their world also meant laughing at tricks, jokes, ventriloquism and disguises. In different books, Fatty posed as a waxworks Napoleon to eavesdrop on a gang of thieves, dressed up as an old balloon woman, as a butcher's boy with red hair, an old tramp, a mysterious foreigner, a French boy with a limp and as a palm reader who read PC Goon's hand and extracted a shilling for a raffle ticket. As early as book three, **The Mystery of the Secret Room**, it was clear that Fatty, who was a born actor as well as a born detective, artist, mathematician, linguist, writer, leader, skier, tennis player and an all-round genius, had a good knowledge of London's theatre land. He attended a show with his mother in that book for his 13th birthday, but conveniently slipped away to buy the props he needed for his first attempt at disguises, which later became a significant part of the series.

Among all of Blyton's characters in her 700 books, Fatty, like George in the Famous Five (who was partly modelled on herself as a girl) stood out. Little has been known about who, if anyone, Fatty was based on and even Gillian Baverstock believed that he was totally "made up". Enid Blyton Society president Tony Summerfield, however, produced a copy of a handwritten letter - (see copy on page 8) - from Enid Blyton, dated July 1962 and written in Dorset, where she holidayed and set some of her "Famous Five" books. The letter was provided to the society by Trevor Bolton. In it, Enid told a group of young fans: "Fatty is based on a rascal of a boy I knew." Who and where remains a mystery, but further insights would be welcomed.

Marlow Parish Church

Stepping back into the Find-Outers' world also means walking beside the Thames River path, catching the London train, boating, exploring a stately mansion such as Cliveden near Taplow or discovering the charms of nearby villages. Many places close to Bourne End open pathways to other writers who lived in the general vicinity. These include Milton, Thomas Gray, G.K. Chesterton, Kenneth Grahame and the Shelleys. Along the way, as the Find-Outers often did, take time to enjoy hot chocolate in winter or to guzzle lemonade and ices in the summer. Or perhaps visit one of the many country pubs full of atmosphere and history, such as *The Red Lion* or *The Spade Oak* which can be found right beside *Old Thatch*.

Enjoy the adventure.

Chapter Two
Stepping through the open door to Peterswood

British-born Canadian resident Graeme Dempsey captured the spirit of the Mystery series, and why its many fans, including Gillian Baverstock, liked it so much when he wrote in *Green Hedges* magazine in December 2000: "For me and many others, there is something magical and overwhelmingly compelling about the Peterswood fiction...

"From the word go, I was involved in the plot of **The Mystery of the Burnt Cottage** and these children had become my friends. I was a fan and today can still attribute much of my blissful childhood to Enid Blyton.

"The Five Find-Outers books have numerous hilarious and memorable highlights within their specific but successful format. Fatty is clearly the hero of all of them, but Blyton carefully and very cleverly devised that the youngest of the five, Bets, also has a crucial share of the action. As Blyton has been accused over the years of being everything from a racist to a sexist to a person who did not write all of her own material, I believe it is necessary to mention that both Daisy and Bets, the female lead characters in the Mystery series, are indeed as much a part of the Five Find-Outers as the three boys, in many cases proving to be every bit as brave and clever (if not more so) as their male counterparts.

"Similarly, the other characters are just as important to each Mystery as Fatty – though he is undoubtedly the leader with his knack for dressing up in an assortment of outrageous disguises, his quick wit, his remarkable

Idyllic Village ... Wooburn Green

The Thames at Bourne End

powers of deduction and his generosity towards others. He very quickly becomes the leader of the five, supplanting Larry who became the original head of the group in the two earlier stories. Fatty is certainly extremely likeable as a character and his pompous tendency to boast about his innumerable talents hardly ever gets to be too irritating. Larry and Pip are quite different in their mannerisms and reactions to things. Larry, for some reason, is much more respectful of girls, his sister Daisy included. Pip, on the other hand, never fails to lay the blame on little Bets, his young sister, though he has no problem recognising Daisy as an equal. Buster, of course, supplies much of the humour throughout the series, as does the rather rotund Mr Theophilus Goon, who always seems to finish far behind the children at the end of each Mystery. So what if such a premise could not exist in the real world? Who cares if smart children outwitting a boob of a bobby could not really happen every time school breaks? This was exactly *why* Blyton's power did not diminish over a 50 year span. Children have always needed an escape from reality, and Blyton provided that escape into a world of pure adventure better than anyone...

"Many a night I can be found snuggled up in a warm bed, with storms raging outside, and the imagined and unimagined dramas of the day unfolded, with a Mystery book in hand. I can step through that open door anytime, and be in the very alive village of Peterswood, on a hot summer's day shut up in Fatty's shed examining "glues" or biking down to the dairy to have another plate of gooey macaroons."[6]

The first book, **The Mystery of the Burnt Cottage**, was set in the fictitious Haycock Lane, which like Coldmoorholme Lane, was on the western side of the village. The Lane had an Inn (The Spade Oak) and ran down to the river and railway line. In the stories, Pip and Bets lived in this lane, in a large red house, and Larry and Daisy lived nearby. In the second book, **The Mystery of the Disappearing Cat,** Fatty's family bought a white house in the same area. In early 2008, the members of the Enid Blyton Society online forum (**www.enidblyton.society.co.uk**) delved into which houses the author might have envisaged as the homes of her main characters.

Mysteries aside, the everyday lives of Fatty, Larry, Daisy, Pip and Bets mirrored the childhood Gillian Baverstock recalled from the 1930s. Like Enid Blyton, Fatty's mother was a keen golfer, reader, bridge player and theatre-goer. "Peterswood was Bourne End, no doubt about it and I recognised quite a number of the places, often by their real names," Gillian said. Even the old police station in the High Street resembles the illustrations of Mr Goon's house in early editions of the books.

Expert at work... Jacky Hawthorne in the Old Thatch garden and the Old Thatch water garden (Pictures: Jacky and David Hawthorne).

Springtime at Burnham Beeches... bluebells beneath the beeches (Picture: Andy Barnard)

The riverside village is prosperous, middle-class commuter territory with some of the UK's most expensive housing outside central London. Bourne End, which now has more than 5000 residents, was much smaller and quieter 60 years ago. While golf, tennis, bridge, boating and reading are still popular, life is busier for most people today. The Mystery books also reflected the ready supply of affordable household help available in the 1940s and 1950s. Each of the children's families had at least two domestic staff – as did Enid Blyton when she lived at *Old Thatch*.

In the books, Peterswood, like Bourne End, drew large crowds to its riverbanks in summer. Gillian recalled that her mother did not allow her to swim in the river, although many children did so with great enjoyment. So did the children in **The Mystery of the Missing Necklace** when Pip complained that the village was "too jolly crowded for anything" because:

> "This hot weather is drawing the people to the river in their hundreds! We get motor-coaches all day long – and down by the river there are all sorts of shows to amuse the people when they tire of the river, or it's raining."[7]

Later, after searching in vain for a mysterious man with one brown eye and one blue eye, the children retreated to the river:

> ...and were soon splashing about happily. Fatty, of course was a very fine swimmer, and could swim right across the river and back. Bets splashed happily in the shallow water. The others swam about lazily just out of their depth.[8]

In contrast, **The Mystery of the Strange Bundle** evoked an English village on mid-winter afternoons. The children had all had flu and Bets, who had recovered, visited Fatty to get away from Pip who had reached the "bad tempered stage". After a lunch of soup, roast chicken and vegetables, Fatty gave Bets one of his Sherlock Holmes detective stories (what else?) to read and settled down for a nap. But Bets falls asleep:

> Except for a log falling into the grate, where a bright fire was burning, there was nothing to be heard. Buster was snoozing in the kitchen, keeping one eye open for the big cat. The cat had to keep a certain distance. One paw over the line and Buster flew at her!

The clock on the mantelpiece ticked on. Half-past two. Three o'clock. It was raining outside, and the afternoon was dark. It would have been too dark for Bets to read if she had been awake. Half-past three. Both Fatty and Bets were perfectly still, and the fire grew rather low.[9]

Then the strange voices began. This was probably the funniest of the stories with Fatty using his newly acquired skill, ventriloquism, to spoof his friends and PC Goon.

A few days later, the children were out and about again:

> They went into the little dairy and sat down at one of the tables there. In the summer they had ice-cold milk there, and ice-creams, or lemonade. In the winter the little shop did a roaring trade in hot milk, cocoa, and hot chocolate.[10]

At that point, they were on the trail of a Mystery that eventuated in Chief Inspector Jenks bringing in a plain-clothes detective from Scotland Yard or the Secret Service. This was the result of the children recovering the clothes of a doll (the Strange Bundle) belonging to a ventriloquist who had worked as an undercover agent for the security forces.

Gillian Baverstock vividly recalled crossing the Thames by the Spade Oak Ferry. The ferry ran from close to the back of *Old Thatch* (the pub beside *Old Thatch* is the *Spade Oak*) to the opposite bank, where Winter Hill, near the village of Cookham, was a favourite picnic spot, especially for afternoon tea and watching the sun set. The open-topped ferry, operated by a boatman until the service closed in 1956 with the advent of more local cars, looked like a row boat. The Find-Outers travelled on it in **The Mystery of the Pantomine Cat** when they wanted to talk to an actor called John James from the local Little Theatre, to find out where he was the previous Friday night when the theatre manager's safe had been robbed.

> "Here's the boat," said Fatty, as the ferryman came rowing across. "I'll pay for every one. It's only tuppence each."....
>
> They got across and made their way over a field and up a steep hill to the top. Fatty chose a place from where they could see the ferry....The spring sun was hot. The cowslips around nodded their yellow heads in the breeze. It was very pleasant up there on the hill. Larry yawned and lay down.[11]

"A certain slant of light on winter" afternoons" on the Thames.

Across the green at Taplow village.

The Thames at Bourne End

Marlow

Enid Blyton also drew on Christmas Hill and other local landmarks in ***The Mystery of the Hidden House.*** In that book, the children were forbidden to look for mysteries after PC Goon complained about their behaviour to their parents. Getting up to mischief as usual, they hatched a plan to make up a "pretend" Mystery to get Mr Goon, and his nephew Ern who was staying with him, "all hot and bothered":

> "Now listen all of you," said Fatty." There are strange lights flashing at night over Christmas Hill."[12]

> ... So, in great glee, the Five Find-Outers and Buster set off up Christmas Hill, taking with them what they thought would do for clues. It was a fine sunny day, but cold, and they got nice and warm going up the hill. Their parents were pleased to see them going out. Nobody liked all the five indoors. Some noisy game always seemed to develop sooner or later.[13]

Enid Blyton had been living in Beaconsfield for 10 years by the time ***The Mystery of the Hidden House*** was published, and her daughter said she borrowed one name from that town for the book. That was a street name – Candlemas Lane – in which Ern threw down clues for the others to find. He threw them out of the window, as he was being driven out of the town by car thieves, who feared the children had discovered their secret lair.

They had, because after developing their "pretend" mystery, Fatty and the others had noticed one or two strange things. Curiosity got the better of them and they decided to investigate further after studying a local map:

> Pip found the map and they took it upstairs. Fatty put his finger on Petersbwood, their village. He traced the way to the mill, up the stream on Christmas Hill. Then he traced another way, alongside another stream, that at first ran near the first one and then went across the fields.[14]

...Fatty made his way to the little bridge across the Bourne. He then walked cautiously along the frosty bank of the stream. Two shadowy figures came out from behind a tree and followed him quietly.[15]

The Bourne is the real name of the small stream which meets the Thames at Bourne End. Slightly downstream, close to Lower Marlow is the Thames' intersection with the River Wye, which rises in Buckinghamshire's Chiltern Hills and flows through the town of High Wycombe. Archaeologists believe the surrounding districts, the fertile Thames and Wye Valleys, have been farmed since at least 3000 BC, while Stone Age exploration of the area could date as far back as 350,000 BC.

Old Thatch in Winter
(Picture: Jacky and David Hawthorne)

Burnham Beeches dormouse (Picture: Andy Barnard)

The Thames

*Autumn leaves at Burnham Beeches
(Picture: Andy Barnard)*

They have their own way of doing things!

Chapter Three
Places real .... and almost real

Turning left out of Coldmoorholme Lane, the main road leads to the nearby riverside town of Marlow. Just a metre or two along the road a street sign showing "Sheepridge Lane," to the right, should catch the eye of a Find-Outer reader. This rural lane, with farmlands on either side, leads to the tiny hamlet of Sheepridge, which featured in several Find-Outer books. In **The Mystery of the Missing Necklace** the children walked over the fields to a second hand shop in Sheepridge in search of old trousers for one of Fatty's disguises. He intended impersonating a deaf old man whom they suspected was passing messages between members of a robber gang.

Towards the end of **The Mystery of the Pantomine Cat,** the children headed to Sheepridge by bus to compare the autographs of an actor from the Peterswood (Bourne End) Little Theatre with those he apparently wrote after a show in Sheepridge. He had given the Sheepridge show at the exact time someone dressed as the pantomime cat had robbed the Little Theatre safe.

Sheepridge Lane has a 400 year-old country pub, *The Crooked Billet*, overlooking the surrounding farmlands. Its atmosphere makes it a great place to stop for lunch, dinner or a drink. At the top of the steep lane is Flackwell Heath, with an elevation of 150m atop one of the Chiltern Hills.

A storybook lane... Coldmoorholme Lane woodland

*Next page: Stop off at a pub with atmosphere-
The Crooked Billet in Sheepridge Lane*

Several real towns were also mentioned in ***The Mystery of the Strange Messages*** as the Find-Outers discussed how to track down a house called 'The Ivies'. The local plod, PC Goon, had been receiving anonymous notes telling him to turn a family called Smith out of the place, and he wrongly blamed the children for the notes:

> "I've looked in the street directory and examined the names there of every house in Peterswood, and I'm sure Goon has too," said Fatty, gloomily. "There isn't a single one called 'The Ivies', not a single one."
>
> "What about Marlow?" said Daisy. "There might be a house called 'The Ivies' there."
>
> "There might. And there might be one in Maidenhead and one in Taplow," said Fatty. "But it would take absolutely ages to look up all the houses in the directory."[16]

Marlow, Taplow and Maidenhead, which Gillian Baverstock confirmed her mother knew well and visited often, are each worth a day out. Of the three, Taplow (Buckinghamshire) is the smallest and quietest, with one traditional English pub, *The Oak and Saw*, facing the large, attractive village green. Taplow has fewer than 1,000 residents, many of whom live in leafy streets in elegant brown/orange brick homes with slate roofs (and the odd thatch), leadlight windows, creeper growing up the walls, multiple chimneys and large, well-tended gardens.

The absence of shops in the village centre keeps traffic light and makes *The Oak and Saw,* with its welcoming open fires in winter, another ideal spot for lunch, dinner or a drink. Taplow has had its own cricket club since 1850 as well as a sailing club. The village station, dating from Victorian times, has direct links to London Paddington (45 minutes away) and west to Oxford (50 minutes), with departures every few minutes at peak times.

Taplow's most famous attraction is the historic mansion Cliveden, the Astor family estate , and setting for the 1960s Profumo scandal. It is now a luxury hotel and restaurant. Novelist and poet Walter de la Mare lived at Hill House in Taplow with his wife and four children from 1925 to 1940. It is located on the road between Bourne End and Taplow, which Enid Blyton knew well as she and her first husband, Hugh Pollock, were regularly driven to Taplow to catch the London train.

A picturesque drive across the Thames from Taplow is the much larger town of Maidenhead with around 70,000 residents in the Royal Borough of Windsor and Maidenhead in the county of Berkshire. These days, it is one of the hubs of England's "silicon corridor" of high-tech industries. The earliest known bridge to connect the two river banks was built in 1280 and archaeologists have traced the district's history back as far as the Iron Age. Maidenhead was recorded in the 11th century Domesday Book as Ellington. Its modern name is probably a combination of a pre-Roman Celtic name for a nearby area, "Mai Dun" and "hythe" meaning wharf. In 1649, King Charles I met his children in the town for the last time before his execution. A plaque in the building which is now a bank, commemorates the event.

Enid Blyton featured Maidenhead in ***The Mystery of Tally-Ho Cottage.*** In that Mystery, the Find-Outers were on the trail of an expensive painting stolen by a couple of "fourth rate film actors", Bill and Gloria Lorenzo. The Lorenzos had been renting a house on the river at Peterswood (Bourne End). According to the newspapers the couple, who were on the run, were spotted at Maidenhead, a report which the Find-Outers discussed in the privacy of a riverside boat:

They all got into the little boat and let it bob under them up and down, up and down, as the waves ran in and out.

"What I can't understand now is why the Lorenzos *came* last night – if it was them – talked to the Larkins, and then went away again," said Fatty. "And where did they come from, in the boat? They must have taken a boat from the opposite bank – or from somewhere further up or down the river..."

"Maidenhead!" said Bets, at once.

"Why yes, of course – Maidenhead!" said Fatty, at once. "What an ass I am! Of course – that's why they *went* to Maidenhead – so they could come here by river."

"Jolly long way to row," said Larry. "Miles!"

"Did they come by motor-boat?" wondered Fatty – and immediately got a clap on the back from Ern.[17]

Later, the Find-Outers proved their suspicions when they spotted the remains of a gold picture frame burning on a bonfire near the Lorenzo's old house, as well as part of a crate with the letters n- h-e- still showing.

Marlow, a pretty riverside town along the Thames path from Bourne End also featured in several books. A bridge has spanned the river there since the early 14th century, with the current suspension bridge built in the late 1820s. Dating from Tudor times, the *George and Dragon* pub, its window boxes a riot of colour against the black and white exterior, is close to the river and its great atmosphere makes it an inviting spot, winter or summer.

The riverside areas of Marlow probably looked very similar years ago when Enid Blyton included the town in several of the Mystery books. Large groups of school students, including a foreign prince who went missing, camped "on the hills between Peterswood and Marlow" in **The Mystery of the Vanished Prince**. In **The Mystery of the Hidden House** Fatty, disguised as Ern Goon, the policeman's nephew, rode to Marlow to check up on a dubious garage owner by the name of Holland. Holland was connected with a mysterious building in the middle of Bourne Wood that later turned out to be a workshop for repainting stolen cars. On a sunny April morning in the Easter holidays in **The Mystery of the Missing Man** Fatty jogged to Marlow along the river path. Later, one of his parents' house guests, Eunice Tolling, became lost in the same area at night:

Above: Marlow Church

Next Page: Remembrance Day Marlow...
outside the George and Dragon
Below: Stoke Park near Stokes Poges
(Picture: Kevin Day)

So off she went shining her torch in front of her. But she was now on the long, long river-path to Marlow, and it seemed as if the way would go on stretching into the swirling mist for ever and ever. Eunice was almost in tears.[18]

In ***The Mystery of Holly Lane***, in which the Find-Outers were on the trail of furniture stolen from an old man, they visited the riverside town to talk to the man's relations and have tea at "that nice little café in Marlow High Street":

> Every one was outside Fatty's gate at three o'clock, Buster included. "I'll have to put him in my bicycle basket," said Fatty. "Marlow's too far for him to go on his four short legs. Up with you Buster!"
>
> Buster liked the bicycle basket. He sat there happily, bumping up and down when Fatty went over ruts. He looked down on other dogs with scorn as he passed them.

> It was about three miles to Marlow, and a very pleasant ride on that fine April day. They asked for Spike Street when they got there. It was a pretty street leading down to the river. No.82 was the last house, and its lawn sloped down into the water.[19]

Later in the story, the three boys, Fatty, Larry and Pip returned to Marlow after a visit to the cinema to see *Ivanhoe*. They travelled to Marlow to track down a horse float where they suspected the old man's grandnephew, Wilfrid, had hidden the stolen furniture. They found it, and freed Wilfrid's cousin, Marian, whom Wilfrid had locked in the float after she had hidden her grandfather's money by sewing it into the hems of his curtains.

As well as using real places as settings, Gillian Baverstock said her mother adapted several other nearby locations. The village of Wooburn Green appeared in the first story in the series, ***The Mystery of the Burnt Cottage,*** as Wilmer Green. Larry and Daisy rode there on the trail of prime suspect Horace Peeks:

> After some hard cycling they came to the village of Wilmer Green. It was a pretty place, with a duck-pond on which many white ducks were swimming. The children got off their bicycles and began to look for Ivy Cottage. They asked a little girl where it was, and she pointed it out to them. It was well set back from the road, and backed on to a wood.[20]

Sheepridge appeared as "Sheepsale market" in ***The Mystery of the Spiteful Letters.*** The Find-Outers caught an early bus there to try to spot who was posting spiteful, anonymous letters from Sheepsale on Monday mornings, market day:

> "....Soon be at Sheepsale now," said Fatty. "Golly, isn't this a steep pull-up?" They saw it wanted eight horses to pull the coach up in the old days before motor buses.[21]

In the same book, Gladys, housemaid to Pip's and Bets' family, the Hiltons, received one of the anonymous letters at their home, Red House. Upset by its contents, she headed to her aunt's place at the hilltop village of "Haycock Heath" – a location Gillian believed was probably based on Flackwell Heath.

Slightly more mysterious was the true location – if it was based on anything real – of the setting for ***The Mystery of Banshee Towers,*** the final book in the Mystery series. Writing in the summer 1996 edition of The Enid Blyton Society Journal, author David Cook commented on a local building - possibly it was near Hedsor - that he believed appeared in several other series: "The route to Taplow from Bourne End goes past a structure on the hillside that Enid cannot fail to have noticed and been inspired by...Viewed from greater distance on the Ferry road between Cookham and Bourne End it is the prototype for the illustration of Torling castle on the dustwrapper spine of hardbacked editions of ***Good Old Secret Seven*** and no doubt under snow, of Old Towers in ***Five Get into a Fix.*** A winding track leads to it up the hillside through trees, and its back is protected by a copse, giving it a very mysterious air."[22]

This mysterious air could also have made it an ideal imaginary setting for the peculiar Banshee Towers on Banshee Hill, to which the Find-Outers set off in high spirits to view sea pictures in an art gallery:

> Soon they were all cycling away down the country lanes, very happy to be going on a picnic to Banshee Hill. The spring sun shone down, the birds sang in the hedges, and the sky was as blue as in summer.[23]

As they reached the summit, the sky and storyline darkened:

> "No, I'm all right," said Daisy panting. "I just hope we get to the top before it pours! I say- that looks a pretty grim place up on the hill, doesn't it?"

Above: A roof to last another 100 years… Old Thatch

Previous page top: Stoke Park
(Picture: Kevin Day)
Previous page below: Bourne End

"Yes - more like an old fortress than anything!" shouted back Fatty. "Look at the two dogs – we've left them far behind! Never mind – they'll catch us up some-time."
They arrived at the gloomy old place at last, and stacked their bicycles in a convenient shed. Then they made their way to the entrance. [24]

And stepped into a peculiar Mystery where a wailing Banshee turned out to be the least of their puzzles…

Chapter Four
Down a storybook lane

Not only was *Old Thatch* a good backdrop for writing children's stories, but Coldmoorholme Lane, 70 years after Enid Blyton packed up her typewriter and moved to Green Hedges in Beaconsfield, still has plenty to offer in the way of story-book settings. There are nearby farms, the Thames with its colourful boats at the bottom of the gardens on the *Old Thatch* side of the lane, The Spade Oak, hedgerows, a railway line beside the river as well as gulls, geese and ducks.

During her years living at *Old Thatch,* Enid Blyton's reputation as a leading children's writer grew. Her output of stories increased year by year and some of her most memorable early characters and books appeared at that time. She was writing regularly for *Teacher's World* magazine and many of her later books, including *Mr Galliano's Circus*, were first published as magazine stories in Enid Blyton's *Sunny Stories* magazine. The first of a trilogy, *Mr Galliano* was published as a novel in 1938. So was *The Secret Island*, a favourite of Gillian Baverstock's, and still regarded as one of the best of Blyton's 700 works. It was the first of five novels about an orphaned farm boy, Jack, and three friends - siblings Peggy, Nora and Mike - who ran away to make a home on an island in a lake, escaping their unpleasant guardians, after their parents were believed to have been killed in an air crash while flying to Australia.

The classic *Adventures of the Wishing Chair,* published in book form in 1937, also began as a *Sunny Stories* magazine series. Still popular with the cyber generation, it was the story of two small children, Mollie and Peter, who sat in an old chair in an antique shop, wished they were at home, and found that the chair sprouted red wings and transported them. The chair stayed in their playroom, taking them on extraordinary adventures, along

Old Thatch (Picture: Jacky and David Hawthorne)

with their new friend, Chinky the Pixie, whom they rescued from slaving as a giant's servant in a castle.

The Three Golliwogs was also written at *Old Thatch*. So were the first, hilarious misadventures of Mister Meddle, the nosy busybody who stumbled through life in a perpetual muddle, infuriating his short-tempered Aunt Jemima and everyone else. Prone to such errors as pouring powerful glue instead of custard over the jam roll for pudding, he was something of an early story-book version of the hapless Frank Spencer in the television series *Some Mothers do Have' Em.*

One of the most popular books written at *Old Thatch* was the first in the Magic Faraway Tree series, *The Enchanted Wood*, which remains a favourite with children around the world. In these stories, three city children, Jo, Bessie and Fanny moved to the country, where the wood near their new home had an extraordinary tree, yielding horse chestnuts and acorns one day and different fruits the next. It was inhabited by magical characters - Moon-Face, Silky the Fairy, Saucepan Man, Dame Washalot, Mr Whatzisname and the Angry Pixie. Together with their new friends, the children visited the strange lands which arrived periodically at the top of the tree. Some of these were frightening, like the mad school of Dame Slap, and some were thrilling, such as the land of snow and ice, toyland or the birthday land.

Some of Gillian Baverstock's fondest memories of *Old Thatch* were of her mother reading her newly-written stories. "Her mind was never still," she recalled. "She could be so entertaining, picking up a doll, speaking in her voice and pretending she was the naughtiest doll in the nursery, upsetting all the other toys, she had us in fits of laughter."

Gillian Baverstock, her dog Bruce and Jacinta Livingstone at IIkley, Yorkshire (Picture: Tess Livingstone)

This was especially the case with a large rag doll Gillian was given as a toddler, Amelia Jane, the "naughty girl" of the *Old Thatch* nursery. Amelia, or so Blyton imagined, snipped tails off toy animals, painted their noses blue, pricked inflatable toys with pins, hid other dolls' shoes and turned on the garden fountain, soaking Gillian's other toys. These, which included a sailor doll, the bear, a golliwog, a clown, a clockwork mouse and several smaller dolls, were at their wits end trying to manage her. Amelia Jane's adventures first appeared in *Sunny Stories* magazine in 1937 and were published in book form the following year.

Gillian herself, her younger sister, Imogen, and several family pets from *Old Thatch*, including Enid's favourite dog, Bobs, appeared in 16 short stories set in Coldmoorholme Lane. *Tales of Old Thatch,* published in 1934/35 and 1938/39, are now collectors' items. In these stories, written for pre-schoolers, Gillian wheeled her dolls around the lane in a pram as she went to buy eggs from the nearby farm and one day returned with an injured lamb in the pram.

She also put up a nesting box for a robin in a tree, but was disappointed when she could no longer find the birds in the garden. Instead, she found the hen-robin building a nest in her dolls' cot in the Wendy house in the garden:

The eggs hatched. Out came four tiny black chicks. Then what a busy time the two robins had! They had to feed their four children all day long! Sometimes Gillian found a grub and fed them too. They weren't a bit afraid of her. Then one day all the baby robins were gone. They had flown out of the window ...[25]

In print, it was an idyllic world where buttercups and daisies flowered and a few pence bought a birthday present at the village shops. Despite her mother's increasingly heavy writing and other work commitments, Gillian recalled *Old Thatch* as a wonderful place for a young child, aside from the vast inconvenience of the odd river flood and rat plague. It was a home she was understandably sad to leave and, despite being just seven years old when her family moved, her memories were vivid. In later years, the care lavished on *Old Thatch* by Jacky and David Hawthorne was a real comfort to Gillian, especially in light of the fact that her second childhood home, *Green Hedges* in Beaconsfield, was torn down after her mother left it.

Chapter Five
Back in the real world

The wider district around Bourne End has much for travellers to explore:

Green Hedges model at Bekonscot

Beaconsfield, Buckinghamshire.
After leaving *Old Thatch* Enid Blyton lived at *Green Hedges*, Beaconsfield for 30 years until shortly before her death in a London nursing home in 1968. Sadly, *Green Hedges*, a red brick house with some black and white gabled walls, was demolished to make way for a new housing estate. A replica of the house was unveiled in 1997 by Gillian Baverstock at *Bekonscot Model Village and Railway,* Warwick Road Beaconsfield. Gillian said she and her mother were frequent visitors to Bekonscot, and her mother set a short story *The Enchanted Village,* there in the 1950s. It began: "Would you like to come with me and visit a village so small that you will tower above the houses? Would you like to know what it would be like if you visited Fairyland, and felt like a giant, because everything was so tiny, and the people hardly came up to your ankles? Well, I live quite near to a little village like this – it is so close that I can see it from my bedroom window. Shall I take you there?"[26]

English country garden
(Picture: Jacky and David Hawthorne)

Now 80 years old, Bekonscot, which started as the backyard hobby of London accountant Roland Callingham in the 1920s, covers 1.5 acres. Bekonscot's model villages, towns, castles, farms, lakes, beaches, zoo, cricket grounds and fairs are linked by the model railway. There is also a ride-on railway for children. More than 13 million visitors have enjoyed the attraction, including the Queen, who was taken there as a child by her grandmother, Queen Mary. Profits go to charity, and more than 5 million pounds have so far been raised. See **www.bekonscot.com**.

Many Beaconsfield residents, including Robert and Tina Massie, whose nearby Red Lion Hotel at Knotty Green has a splendid Enid Blyton Room, believe that Enid Blyton's famous Noddy/Toytown books were inspired by the Bekonskot model village. It has the same "feel" as Toytown and it is a "must visit" attraction for children. Even the most sophisticated adults would admire the craftmanship and detail of the enterprise.

Bekonscot
(Picture: Jacinta Livingstone)

Directly across the road from Bekonscot is the car park of St Teresa's Catholic Church, the Parish church of one of England's most famous literary converts, G.K. Chesterton. Chesterton moved to Beaconsfield in 1909, and lived there with his wife until his death in June 1936. One of the statues in the church, Our Lady holding the infant Jesus, was given by Chesterton and the Martyrs Chapel is a memorial to him. See **www.littleflower.co.uk**. Chesterton's house, *Top Meadow* in Grove Road, is privately owned and carries a blue plaque in his memory.

Inside the Red Lion pub
(Picture: Tina and Bob Massie)

Bletchley Park
The Bletchley Park, Bletchley, Milton Keynes, Buckinghamshire, (beside Bletchely station)

BRITISH wartime Prime Minister Winston Churchill called Bletchley Park "the goose that laid the golden egg but never cackled."
Fortunately, for the benefit of visitors, the stately mansion and adjacent huts where 12,000 code breakers, wireless operators and support staff worked around the clock during World War II in total secrecy, looks much as it did in Churchill's day.

The desks and equipment used by the thousands of wireless operators who carefully noted every letter or figure as they tracked enemy radio nets are preserved. The rooms and huts in which they worked also contain wartime maps, decor and furniture.

Bletchley Park

Plenty of attention is given to the extraordinary mathematical geniuses whose electronic expertise created the machines that cracked the German's use of the Enigma cipher machine, believed by the Germans to be secure. The codebreakers' work shortened the war and saved countless lives, cutting German supply lines, wreaking havoc on the Luftwaffe and German navy and assisting the Americans, later in the war, to apply similar pressure to the Japanese.

Especially fascinating, in light of today's technology, is Colossus, the world's first programmable electronic computer built at Bletchley in 1943 to track German defences in Europe in the lead up to D Day the following year. In 1991, Bletchley Park, by then in disrepair and set to be bulldozed to make way for a housing estate, was the scene of a farewell party for 400 former staff. It was there the decision was made to restore the site and the Bletchley Park Trust, with the Duke of Kent as patron, was formed.

Queen Victoria would come for tea... Cliveden near Taplow

Cliveden

They have done a brilliant job, and a visit to the centre can easily fill a day – or a week for the real enthusiasts - especially if it's fine enough for picnics by the lake, beside the croquet lawn. The ideal starting point is the museum and its films, beside the entrance and shop. Bletchley is open year round, see **www.bletchleypark.org.uk.**

The Chilterns. Bordered by the Thames in the south, the Chiltern Hills was designated as an Area of Outstanding Natural Beauty in 1965. It takes in the gently rolling woodland hills, chalk downlands and villages of much of Buckinghamshire and Oxfordshire, as well as parts of Bedfordshire and Hertfordshire. It is worth taking time to drive, cycle or walk around the region to appreciate the wildlife, the scenery and the strong sense of history. This is derived from the Norman churches and brick and flint cottages in village after village, many of them predating the Domesday Book. A few days in this environment, in a landscape that lives and breathes centuries rather than the hurly burly of today's 24/7 pace, engenders a calm sense of living history and the passage of time.

Cliveden. Taplow, Berkshire. In a setting of 376 acres of stunning National Trust gardens and parklands, Cliveden, these days, is one of the world's grandest stately hotels. The current mansion is the 3rd that has stood on the site since 1666 and the mansion's visitors books are a who's who of history spanning centuries. Those who have visited include monarchs, Prime Ministers, US Presidents, writers and film stars, not to mention the main players in the 1960s Profumo scandal.

Queen Victoria, a frequent guest, was reportedly not amused in 1893 when the house was bought by William Waldorf Astor, America's richest citizen. When he gave it to his son and daughter-in-law - the indefatigable Nancy Astor, Westminster's first female MP in 1906 - Cliveden became the hub of a hectic social whirl where guests included everyone from Charlie Chaplin to Winston Churchill, and President Roosevelt to George Bernard Shaw.

Cookham Dean, Berkshire. Directly across the Thames from Cliveden is the village of Cookham, childhood home of *Wind in the Willows* author, Kenneth Grahame, who lived with his grandmother at *The Mount*, now Herries School.

Chalfont St Giles. Buckinghamshire.
"Laurel and Myrtle and what higher grew Of firm and fragrant leaf: on either side Acanthus, and each odourous bushy shrub Fenc'd up the verdant wall, each beauteous flower, Iris all hues, Roses and Jessamine Reard high their flourish'd beads between, and wrought Mosaic."

Roald Dahl

So wrote John Milton in Paradise Lost, Book 4, Line 694, completed in his timber-framed brick cottage in Chalfont St Giles in 1667 after he escaped London's plague. The cottage and garden, with many of the plants Milton mentioned in his poetry, is now the Milton Museum, open from March to October. See **www.miltonscottage.org**. The village is also worth seeing for its 12th century Norman Church, village green duck pond and early Quaker meeting house where one of the founding fathers of the United States, William Penn, is buried.

Great Missenden. A Buckinghamshire village in the Chiltern Hills, Great Missenden was home to children's author Roald Dahl, who lived and wrote at Gipsy House in the village from 1954 until his death in 1990. In 2005, the Roald Dahl Museum and Story Centre opened in the High Street, which had been the setting for one or two Dahl stories. It was looking across the

Cookham

High Street from her bedroom window that Sophie first spotted the BFG (Big Friendly Giant) lumbering through the village in one of Dahl's most popular stories. The Centre is a fine celebration of his life, with plenty of films, manuscripts and memorabilia on display, including his desk light and pencils. Different rooms are dedicated to stories like *Charlie and the Chocolate Factory, Matilda, Fantastic Mr Fox, The BFG* and *James and the Giant Peach*. Along with his school reports, there is also Dahl's RAF log from his days as a World war II fighter pilot. Budding authors have the chance to sit in the great man's 'really comfy' writing chair, and join in interactive games and activities. The Centre is dedicated to giving children the chance to develop their own creative writing potential. Open year round, the museum's website is **www.roalddahlmuseum.org**. Pushing on through the Chilterns region, the picturesque market town of Amersham is just a 15 minute drive away. Amersham, dating back to pre-Saxon times, is linked to London 27 miles away by Underground, as the last stop on the Metropolitan railway line. It might seem familiar to many, as parts of the movie *Four Weddings and a Funeral* and several episodes of *Midsomer Murders* were filmed there.

Royal Ascot. Ascot Berkshire. Aside from the five-day Royal Ascot meeting in June attended by the Royal Family, horse racing – both on the flat and with jumps – is held at Ascot throughout the year, attracting 500,000 visitors. Even for non-gamblers it's a colourful, interesting experience in a pretty part of the country, close to Windsor. See **www.ascot.co.uk**

Stoke Poges. South-east Buckinghamshire, 23 miles west of Hyde Park corner.

> "The Curfew tolls the knell of parting day,
> The lowing herd winds slowly o'er the lea,
> The ploughman homeward plods his weary way,
> And leaves the world to darkness and to me...".

So wrote Thomas Gray in his famous 1750 *Elegy Written in a Country Churchyard*. Gray is buried at St Giles Church, Stoke Poges, where the poem is believed to have been written. Still a working Parish church, St Giles is at least 1,000 years old, combining Saxon, Norman, and early Gothic and Tudor architecture. Its history and uplifting, other-worldly feel make it fascinating in its own right, aside from the fact that one of the most memorable poems in the English language was composed there.

Just 1.5 miles from the gates of St Giles is **Burnham Beeches**, the breathtakingly beautiful forest which is at its best whatever the season. Whether its grounds are snow covered in winter, leaf-covered in autumn, bluebell-covered in spring or green and lush in summer, a walk through Burnham Beeches is unforgettable. The average age of its vast, craggy pollarded beech trees is 400 years, with one of the largest trees in the woodland, known as Druid's Oak, with a girth of 30 feet around the trunk, believed to be 800 years old. If trees ever looked like they had personalities, it is these. It is also possible, on quiet days, to spot fauna such as a dormouse dozing in a tree hollow or a baby muntjac, an ancient breed of deer.

St. Giles Stoke Poges and its churchyard in winter
(Picture: Kevin Day)

Stonor Park. Stonor Park, Henley-on-Thames, Oxfordshire. Located between the M4 and M40 on the B480 Henley-on-Thames - Watlington Road, five miles north of Henley.

As sunshine steams in through the stained glass window behind the altar of the Blessed Trinity Chapel at Stonor Park, it's easy to feel overwhelmed by the historic significance of the surrounds. Stonor is a private family chapel but welcomes visitors of all denominations for the 10.30 am Sunday Mass. It has belonged to the Stonor family since the 13th century. Set in rolling countryside five miles north of Henley-on-Thames, Stonor was a site of Catholic resistance during the English Reformation.

St Edmund Campion, the martyred Jesuit who was captured at Lyford Grange (still a working farmhouse) near Wantage in Oxfordshire, often visited Stonor. One of his most famous books, the *Ten Reasons for Being a Catholic* (sufficient to earn him a grisly death at Tyburn after torture in the Tower of London) was printed in the attic roof of the house in 1581.

St. Edmund's Campion's hideout - Stonor (Picture: Tess Livingstone

The house, gardens (complete with pre-historic stone circle), art collection and chapel are open to visitors on Sundays and some weekdays from April to September, and the chapel is open for the Sunday Mass throughout the year.

Thousands of golden daffodils make Easter weekend at Stonor something special. Reportedly, it is an ideal place for spotting Red Kites, a rare and beautiful bird found in the Chiltern countryside. Stonor is also home to Buzzards, Green Woodpeckers and several species of owl, all of which have thrived in the tranquillity and safety of the ancient grounds. See **www.stonor.com.**

Just up the road from the estate is the popular 14th century *Crown Inn* pub with its own "priest's hole" - used when hiding out at Stonor became too dangerous. On a cold January morning after Mass, we rated its hot chocolate "the best ever".

A pub with a priest's hole... and a terrific chef.
The Crown Inn, Pishill, near Stonor
(Picture: Tess Livingstone)

Windsor. Leave the M4 Motorway at Junction 6 to explore Windsor Castle and St George's Chapel, both open to the public. So is nearby Windsor Great Park, with its thousands of acres of riding and walking trails. It has a manmade lake - Virginia Water - and the former royal residence, Frogmore, has art works by Queen Victoria and her children on display. Queen Victoria so loved the place that she and Prince Albert are buried in a mausoleum in the Frogmore grounds. For opening times see **www.royal.gov.uk** and follow the links. Visitors – including colonials – do not need royal blood to enjoy the produce from the Royal Farms. A variety of produce including beef and dairy products from the royal herds, hand-made chocolate fudge and honey is available at the Windsor Farm shop, Datchet Road, Old Windsor. See **www.windsorfarmshop.co.uk** for details. It's even possible – and highly enjoyable – to spend an hour or two horse riding in Windsor Great Park. Contact Tally Ho Stables, Tally Ho Farm, Crouch Lane, Windsor. **www.tallyhostables.co.uk**. An easy walk across the bridge from Windsor is the town of Eton. Eton College, founded in 1440 by King Henry VI, is the alma mater of 19 British Prime Ministers and has 1300 boarding school boys aged 13 to 18. The school, including its magnificent chapel, is open for tours at certain times, see **www.etoncollege.com**. It is impossible to remain unmoved by the honour rolls of Etonians who died in the world wars - 1157 in World War I and 748 in World War II. Junction 6 of the M4 is also the motorway exit for Legoland Windsor, a theme park which children will find magical. The park has more than 50 rides, shows and attractions. One of the most popular is the "driving school", allowing 6 to 13 year olds to earn their "licence" to steer electric cars around a course with traffic lights, roundabouts and other drivers. See **www.legoland.co.uk**.

Legoland (Picture: Jacinta Livingstone)

A child's dream come true... Legoland near Windsor (Picture: Tess Livingstone)

Chapter Six
Hidden Treasure

As sixpences go, it was a rare find. Working in their garden at *Old Thatch* one day, close to the back door, Jacky and David Hawthorne came across a small, discoloured object that turned out to be a silver sixpence, dating from 1696. Was it a one-off discovery or a sign of hidden treasures? Nobody knows for sure, which is part of the charm of a home with close to 400 years history. The five Find-Outers would have been fascinated.

Enid Blyton, who also used to find centuries-old coins while working in *Old Thatch* garden, believed the house had a hidden cellar concealing books, letters and treasure from the mid-Victorian era, "the savings of two old women who had once kept the inn. They had put their money into a box and had hidden it so safely that when they died no one could ever find it though many searched for days!"[27]

She was also fascinated by the legend of the *Old Thatch* "ghost" – that of a horse that had lived in the stables and purportedly galloped around the house once a year in January looking for its former stables. Even today, the old hasps where the stable doors were hung are visible. One horse that probably was stabled at *Old Thatch* in the early 18th century was Black Bess, belonging to infamous highwayman Dick Turpin, whom Enid Blyton believed had used *Old Thatch* – then an alehouse – as one of his boltholes after robbing travellers on the Bath Road at Maidenhead Thicket.

Jacky and David Hawthorne noticed *Old Thatch* for sale while out for a walk one evening, and bought the house well aware that as a Grade 2 heritage listed building its outside could not be changed. That was not a problem. "It's a cosy, distinctive house. It's perfect" Jacky said.

Jacky, who read and enjoyed *Noddy* and *The Secret Seven* as a child, was not a Blyton fanatic. However she and David have accepted the interest in the *Old Thatch*/Blyton connection with good humour and enjoy chatting with British, American, Australian and other visitors who come to see the garden on open days. These visitors in late spring and summer can enjoy the atmosphere of the home along with tea and "homemade scrummy cake" – usually carrot cake or chocolate slice. The tea room is at the back of the house, with French doors leading out to a paved terrace with tables and chairs overlooking the cottage garden. The Hawthornes originally opened the house one day a year to help raise money for charity. This practice continues. Later, they extended the opening times and around 2000 visitors generally come through in a season.

Over the years, the Hawthornes have made *Old Thatch* more comfortable inside, while retaining its important traditional features such as the dining room's elegant leadlight windows, its oak beams taken from wooden ships and a vast, welcoming fireplace. Enid Blyton described the fireplace in *The Story of My Life* as*:* "so big and wide that a man could easily stand upright in it. It has come into many of my tales – with secret hiding places added to it!"[28]

The Hawthornes also transformed the garden, which was in much need of some "tender loving care". Jacky, a landscape gardener and David, shared the work. While retaining the garden's traditional features including Enid Blyton's round pond and the centuries-old well, they have given the garden structure, creating different areas that are in sharp contrast with each other, while blending together into a coherent whole.

In the many and varied chapters of its colourful past, it is fair to say that *Old Thatch* gardens have never looked better. From the freshness of spring and the high colours and multiple greens of summer to the rich russet hues of autumn, *Old Thatch* gardens have a different personality across the seasons. Never is this more evident than in deep midwinter when the bare trees and thatched roof stand out against the stark whiteness of surrounding snow under an icy sky.

The various components of the *Old Thatch* garden include a cottage garden with traditional plants such as mallow, delphinium, larkspur, sweet William and poppies spilling onto paths and terraces. There is also a formal garden where box hedging is pierced by standards of ilex and viburnum, a rose walk, a lavender garden where alliums arrive in spring and stand tall and spherical until the lavender takes over in summer. In another part of the garden, water flows over a wide shallow bowl into the deep pool below. The two acres of different areas are linked by various paths and vistas.

Various garden pots, a bird bath, a fountain, a sundial, a coach light and a planted arbour overflowing with scented roses and studded with clematis of all sizes and colours, add variety. Some areas are a riot of colour, while others are dominated by a single colour such as blue or pink. The garden is surrounded by trees, giving it a secluded, sheltered feel. The traditional wooden seats here and there are ideal for reading or just enjoying the atmosphere. Some of its charms have been televised when *Old Thatch* was used as a setting for the home of a barrister on Kavanagh QC, starring the late John Thaw.

Interesting plantings and combinations of plants in the *Old Thatch* garden underline Jacky's knowledge of what grows well in the area. At any one time, Jacky's studio in-tray is packed with 14 or more garden projects on which she is engaged around Buckinghamshire, Berkshire, Oxfordshire and west London as she increasingly makes her mark as one of the south of England's most skilled and distinguished garden designers. The proof of that moniker rests with *Old Thatch*'s one star rating in the Telegraph Good Gardens Guide. To put the honour in context locally, Cliveden's 376 acres, tended by teams of gardeners, has two stars. Increasingly, *Old Thatch* is establishing an international reputation and each year receives visitors from all round the world, including horticultural tours from mainland Europe.

As well as designing and overseeing the creation or revitalisation of gardens large and small, Jacky is available to advise on solutions to particular garden problems. She also leads several seminars a year on garden plantings at *Old Thatch*, where the garden is used to provide practical examples. Several "painting days" a year are also held giving experienced and amateur artists the chance to find a corner of the garden, be inspired and set to work on their picture – be it a detailed portrait of one stunning flower or a wider landscape taking in house and garden. For details and dates see **www.jackyhawthorne.co.uk**.

In the ongoing life of *Old Thatch,* the Hawthornes have shaped the home and certainly the garden as much as or even more than any of its previous owners through four centuries. And *Old Thatch*, in turn, has shaped their lives as well, albeit in a different creative direction to the one it shaped Enid Blyton's life and career.

As the author recalled decades after moving on from Coldmoorholme Lane: "It was a lovely place to write stories in, that four hundred-year-old cottage...you will understand why I loved it so much, and why I remember it so well. Look at it – you will be sure to recognise it in many of my books!"[29]

Enid Blyton's favourite garden statue which she took to "Green Hedges" from "Old Thatch". Gillian later moved it to Yorkshire.

Enid Blyton
(Picture: Tess Livingstone)

Acknowledgements

GRATEFUL thanks to the owners of *Old Thatch*, Jacky and David Hawthorne, for their cheerful co-operation with this project. Enid Blyton would salute their expertise in improving *Old Thatch* and its gardens, making them – officially – among the best in Britain.

The outstanding photographic talents of London lawyer Matthew Rose – an old friend from Brisbane – captured the beauty of these places better than thousands of words ever could, as do Andy Barnard's excellent pictures of Burnham Beeches and Kevin Day's images of Stoke Poges. The four-seasonal beauty of that part of England has no limits. Thank you, also, Tina and Bob Massie for the pictures of the Red Lion at Knotty Green, Beaconsfield and for giving such a popular author her due in the Enid Blyton Room.

A very big thank you to publishers Anthony and Brigid Cappello, whose entrepreneurial flair and determination have made Connor Court such a dynamic Australian publisher. I am also grateful to Pam Alley, Esra Cafer and Danella Taylor at Chorion in London, custodians of Enid Blyton's literary estate. I am indebted to Tony Summerfield, organiser extraordinaire of the Enid Blyton Society, and to my fellow members for their website of interesting stories, snippets and insights. If you enjoyed this book you would enjoy the society. See **www.enidblytonsociety.co.uk**.

Although this book was written in the second half of 2007, most of the research was completed while we were living in the UK in 2002. That happy time included a memorable winter's morning when my daughter, Jacinta, then on holiday from primary school in London, and I visited Mrs Gillian Baverstock, Enid Blyton's elder daughter in Ilkley, Yorkshire.

As Jacinta marvelled at the chance to sit at Enid Blyton's writing table ("Imagine, this is where Moon Face, Saucepan Man and Silky were born") Gillian poured out her crystal clear memories of growing up in Bourne End, her knowledge of the Mystery series and its locales and much else about her mother. Her insights were fascinating and invaluable. Sadly, Gillian died in June 2007. She was a brilliant, generous lady.

Now in her last year of secondary school at Brisbane Girls Grammar School, I would like to thank Jacinta for her excellent proof reading and for meandering around the riverside villages of the Thames Valley with me.

Finally, this book is dedicated with affection to our dear friends, Gail Wiltshire and her niece, Elley Raymond. From *The Three Golliwogs* to Tennyson, *Peter Pan* to Shakespeare, sharing Jacinta's and Elley's journey from fairyland to literature, enhanced by Gail's encyclopaedic knowledge and vibrant teaching skills, has added extraordinary enjoyment to countless school holidays.

www.ingramcontent.com/pod-product-compliance
Lightning Source LLC
Chambersburg PA
CBHW050504110426
42742CB00018B/3367